D1716660

★ ★

EXPLORERS OF AMERICA

Leif Ericson
EXPLORER OF VINLAND

MATTHEW G. GRANT
Illustrated by Dick Brude

GALLERY OF GREAT AMERICANS SERIES

★ ★

Leif Ericson
EXPLORER OF VINLAND

Library of Congress Number: 73-14531   ISBN: 0-87191-278-3

Published by Creative Education, Mankato, Minnesota 56001
Distributed by Childrens Press, 1224 West Van Buren Street, Chicago, Illinois 60607

LIBRARY OF CONGRESS CATALOGING IN PUBLICATION DATA
Grant, Matthew G
    Leif Ericson; explorer of Vinland.
    (Explorers in America) (Gallery of great American series)
    SUMMARY: A brief account of the life and discoveries of the Norse explorer who became one of the first white men to visit America.
    1. Leiv Eiriksson, d. ca. 1020—Juvenile literature. [1. Ericson, Leif, d. ca. 1020. 2. Explorers, Norse. 3. American—Discovery and exploration] I. Keely, John, illus. II. Title: Explorer of Vinland.
E105.G76   973.1'3'0924 [B] [92]   73-14531
ISBN 0-87191-278-3

CONTENTS

VIKING BOY OF ICELAND

In the year 960, a Norwegian man named Thorvald committed murder. He and his grown son, Eric the Red, fled the island of Iceland. At the time, many Norse people lived there.

In spite of its cold-sounding name, Iceland was a pleasant place. Warm sea currents kept it from getting too cold. The ocean around it was full of fish. Thousands of Viking people had come there from Norway and settled. They raised barley and had sheep, goats, cattle, and poultry.

Ships from Iceland traveled the North Atlantic. Sometimes they traded—and sometimes they raided.

Eric the Red married a wealthy woman named Thorhild. They had sons named Leif, Thorvald, and Thorstein. The boys helped care for the animals on the farm. And like all young Vikings, they became good sailors.

When Leif was still a boy, his father got into trouble. About 985 he killed two men. The people decided to banish Eric for three years, but his family was allowed to stay in Iceland.

Eric said farewell to Thorhild and the boys. He said: "I will sail westward. Some men say there are islands out there. If I find them, I will come back and get you."

For three years the family waited. They feared Eric had died, but he returned during the third summer.

"I have found a new land," Eric told them. "It has green fields. We are going to settle there."

Eric called his discovery Greenland. He gave it a nice name so that other people would join him in settling there. He did not tell the people that most of Greenland was capped by ice, that it had few trees, and that the only soil was thin and rocky.

Iceland was getting crowded, so several hundred people agreed to go with Eric to Greenland. Some 25 ships set out. Only 14 arrived safely.

THE GREENLAND COLONY

In those days, the climate of Greenland was warmer than it is now. A giant glacier lay inland. But near the shore there was grassy land for pastures and small farms. The people built homes and settled down.

Eric and his family had the biggest homestead, since he was the leader. It was called Brattalid and was like a small village with houses for Eric's slaves and many followers. Nine Viking chiefs settled in lands not far away, while others sailed further up the coast.

No Eskimos lived in Greenland at that time. The Vikings were alone in a new land. Only their ships linked them with faraway Europe.

The Greenland winter was very harsh. The sea froze and the people and livestock had to stay indoors. But during the summer it was warm. The women and the children tended gardens and made hay. The men sailed up Greenland's western coast and hunted walrus, seals, and whales. The ivory tusks of the walrus were very valuable. They were to be traded to the markets of Europe, bringing wealth to the Greenland people.

LEIF THE LUCKY

Eric's son, Leif, grew up as the Greenland colony prospered. In the year 997, when Leif was a man, Eric decided to send him to Norway. Leif took a ship loaded with presents to King Olaf.

Norway's king was pleased with the gifts and became fond of Leif. He converted the young man to the Christian religion and gave him a command:

18

"Leif, I want you to preach Christianity in Greenland. I can tell you are a lucky man. The people will listen to you and turn from the fierce old gods to the gentle Christ."

Leif promised to follow the king's command.

On the way home, Leif's ship was blown off-course by a storm. Luckily they came to no harm. They reached an unknown land west of Greenland. Leif said: "Some day we will return here."

They sailed for Greenland. Near home, they rescued some sailors from a wreck. This was thought to be very lucky. The Vikings began to call Leif "Lucky." The name was a symbol of their regard for him.

Because of Leif's preaching, the Greenland people became Christians. The colony grew larger. But there was one serious lack: wood. Only small, scrubby trees grew in Greenland. They were not large enough to use in building houses or ships.

Leif remembered the western land he had visited so briefly. He decided to look for it again and gathered 35 brave men to go with him.

They put out to sea. The first landfall they made was probably barren Baffin Island, just west of Greenland. Leif named the place Helluland—Land of Rock Slabs. It seemed worthless, so they sailed south.

The next place they visited was heavily forested. "We will call this Markland—Land of Woods," Leif said. It was probably the coast of Labrador.

The wind was right, so they kept sailing south.

Two days running before the wind brought them to another place. The Vikings sailed up a

river and cast out their anchor. Leif stepped ashore. He looked happily around at the green grass, trees, and flowers. There were large salmon in the rivers. They found footprints of a large deer, which promised meat.

"We will spend the winter here," Leif said. "I name this place Vinland—Land of Meadows."

VIKINGS IN VINLAND

Historians cannot agree on the location of Leif's Vinland. It may have been Newfoundland, where some ancient Viking ruins have been found. Or Leif may have strayed as far south as Massachusetts.

Next spring, perhaps in the year 1001, Leif sailed back to Greenland. He never returned to the land he had found. Eric the Red died and Leif became the busy ruler of the Greenland colony.

Leif's brother Thorvald explored Vinland next. He was certainly somewhere in America, for he was killed by an Indian arrow after exploring for some months. His crew brought the sad news back to Leif.

For the next 12 years or so, Greenlanders would explore and even try to colonize Vinland. A captain named Thorfinn Karlsefni made a settlement and traded with the Indians. But the red men became hostile and the Vikings had to abandon their new colony, which was probably in Newfoundland.

Leif's half-sister, Freydis, also tried to found a colony. She, too, failed.

Little more is known for certain about the Vikings in Vinland or about Leif Ericson. The Greenland colony lasted until the 1400's when the climate became much colder and the Vikings abandoned the place.

Memories of Vinland were kept alive by the storytellers of Iceland. Their tales became widely known. They may have inspired other Europeans to sail westward in search of a New World.

★ ★
GALLERY OF GREAT AMERICANS SERIES
★ ★

INDIANS OF AMERICA
- GERONIMO
- CRAZY HORSE
- CHIEF JOSEPH
- PONTIAC
- SQUANTO
- OSCEOLA

EXPLORERS OF AMERICA
- COLUMBUS
- LEIF ERICSON
- DeSOTO
- LEWIS AND CLARK
- CHAMPLAIN
- CORONADO

FRONTIERSMEN OF AMERICA
- DANIEL BOONE
- BUFFALO BILL
- JIM BRIDGER
- FRANCIS MARION
- DAVY CROCKETT
- KIT CARSON

WAR HEROES OF AMERICA
- JOHN PAUL JONES
- PAUL REVERE
- ROBERT E. LEE
- ULYSSES S. GRANT
- SAM HOUSTON
- LAFAYETTE

WOMEN OF AMERICA
- CLARA BARTON
- JANE ADDAMS
- ELIZABETH BLACKWELL
- HARRIET TUBMAN
- SUSAN B. ANTHONY
- DOLLEY MADISON

★ ★

DATE DUE		BORROWER'S NAME	ROOM NO.
OCT 4 1976			
APR 1 3 1977		L. Chirstley	18
FEB 4 1981		D. McGuire	29
		Mezer	41